P9-DCR-643

Can you see

a squirrel,

a camel,

and a sow?

CAN YOU SEE WHAT I SEE?
ANIMALS
READ-AND-SEEK

WALTER WICK

SCHOLASTIC INC.

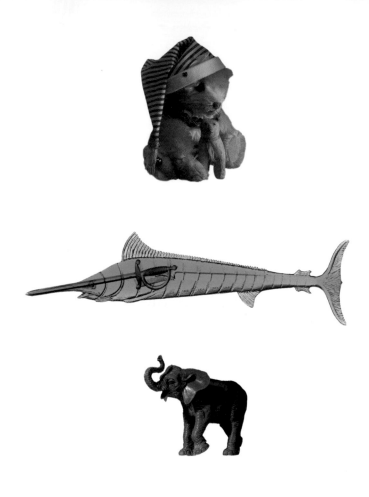

Text copyright © 2007 by Walter Wick.
"Wood Shop," "Picture Blocks," "In Bins," "Alphabet Maze," "Spare Parts," and "See-Through" from *Can You See What I See?* © 2002 by Walter Wick; "Rise and Shine" from *Can You See What I See? Dream Machine* © 2003 by Walter Wick; "Plush Passions," "Animal Kingdom," "Button Fancy," and "Traffic Jam" from *Can You See What I See? Cool Collections* © 2004 by Walter Wick; "A Long Winter's Nap" from *Can You See What I See? The Night Before Christmas* © 2005 by Walter Wick.

All rights reserved. Published by Scholastic Inc.
SCHOLASTIC, CARTWHEEL BOOKS, and associated logos are trademarks and/or registered trademarks of Scholastic Inc.

Library of Congress Cataloging-in-Publication Data

Wick, Walter.
Can you see what I see? Animals read-and-seek / Walter Wick.
p. cm. -- (Scholastic reader. Level 1)
ISBN 0-439-86227-2
1. Picture puzzles--Juvenile literature. I. Title. II. Title: Animals read-and-seek.
GV1507.P47.W5115 2007
793.73--dc22   2006101858

ISBN-13: 978-0-439-86227-1
ISBN-10: 0-439-86227-2

26 25 24 23   40   19/0
Printed in the U.S.A. • First printing, May 2007

Dear Reader,

Read the words and find the hidden objects. For
an extra challenge, cover the picture clues at the
bottom of each page with your hand.

Have fun!

Walter Wick

Can you see

a wolf,

a tiger,

a cow?

Can you see

2 lions,

a panda,

a moose?

Can you see

a penguin,

a mouse,

and a goose?

Can you see

2 rabbits,

a bear,

and a frog?

Can you see

a rooster,

a dinosaur,

and a dog?

Can you see

a fox,

a starfish,

2 bats?

Can you see

3 elephants,

2 fish,

and 2 cats?

Can you see

a swan

and 4 yellow

ducks?

Can you see

a cow

and 2 ducklings

on trucks?

Can you see

2 fish,

an owl,

and a monkey?

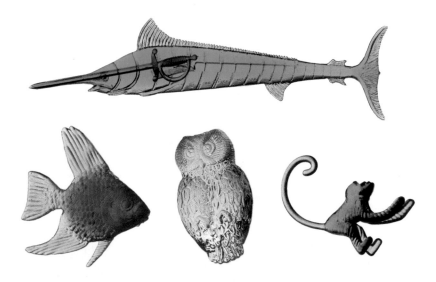

Can you see

2 bears,

a lamb,

and a donkey?

bat

bear

camel

cat

cow

dinosaur

dog

donkey

duckling

elephant

fish

fox

frog

goose

lamb

lion

monkey

moose

mouse

owl

panda

 penguin

rabbit

rooster

sow

 squirrel

starfish

swan

tiger

wolf

yellow duck